GW01606046
Presented to
SUZANNE PRICE
FOR GOOD ATTENDANCE
DURING 1974 AT
WEST VIEW BAPTIST
SUNDAY SCHOOL.
PICKERING & INGLIS LTD.
PRINTED IN GREAT BRITAIN

THE HOUSE THAT DIED

By the same author:

GINGER AND THE V.C.

ACORN BOOKS No 22

THE HOUSE THAT DIED

by

CHRISTINE WOOD

VICTORY PRESS
LONDON and EASTBOURNE

Reprinted 1970

SBN 85476 075 X

For Beryl

Printed in Great Britain by
Compton Printing Ltd.
London and Aylesbury

CONTENTS

Chapter 1

ORMOND GRANGE

Aunt Nancy, who had invited me to stay for the summer holiday, had tea all ready when I arrived, so I left my unpacking until later. I meant to do it straight after tea but my cousin John stopped me.

"I'm going round to see Philip Taylor. Coming?" he said.

"Philip Taylor, who's that?" I asked.

"My friend at *Ormond Grange*. You must remember Pip and Anna from when you were here before. Anna's grown into a lanky, little kid but she's still got that thick, black pony tail. She's just had her tenth birthday and isn't such a scatterbrain as she used to be."

"Oh, Pip and Anna! I was going to ask if you were still friends with Pip. I'd like to see him and Anna again. We had some fun at the old Grange where they live, didn't we?"

Pip, like John, was much taller than when I last saw him but he grinned boyishly enough as he hailed us from the shed where he was cleaning his bicycle. Pip had a round face covered with freckles and he was as jolly as he looked. He was the ideal friend for John who, nice as he was, tended to be rather serious. He went to church every Sunday and was very earnest about it, but Pip, I thought, would stop him from getting too religious.

Pip and I had hardly spoken to each other when Anna came running up. She stopped and stared shyly when she saw me.

"This is Helen. She stayed with John two years ago but I don't suppose you remember," Pip said.

"Yes I do. We played hide-and-seek and she hid behind the hen coop. I could see her head over the top and wished that my hair was fair and pretty like hers."

"There, a compliment for you," Pip said, grinning at me.

"Perhaps we'll play hide-and-seek again and I'll find a better place to hide," I said to Anna.

"But we won't. It's too awful!" came the dramatic reply, and Anna covered her face with her hands and burst into tears.

"Don't cry, silly. We can easily play something else if you'd rather," I said in dismay.

"Not here, we can't," Anna choked. "We've got to move and we've nowhere to go. It's being pulled down."

"Pulled down! What—*Ormond Grange*?" I asked.

Anna nodded sadly as I turned to look at the lovely, old house. My gaze took in the friendly, red brickwork, the quaint, mullioned windows and even quainter gabled chimneys. I saw, too, the fresh green of the Virginia creeper and remembered when I had seen it before —all ablaze in many shades of red and gold.

"What a shame," I said. "Who says the house has got to be pulled down?"

"A man," Anna replied.

"You see, Miss Ormond can't afford to keep it going any more," Pip said more explicitly, "so she's sold it to a Mr. Randall. He's a jam maker and he's having a new factory built here. It's extra to the factory he's already got at the other end of the town."

"But isn't part of the Grange let off into flats?" I asked.

"It was, and we're still in the ground floor one although Dad isn't the gardener here any more," Pip went on. "Miss Ormond said it would have cost her hundreds of pounds to have the roof re-tiled alone. It was too much worry for her, so she sold the house and everyone's moved but us. Miss Ormond's living in a private room in Oaklands Old People's Home, but we can't find anywhere to go and Dad hasn't got another job yet."

"I'm ever so sorry," I said. "I remember Miss Ormond; she was such a sweet, old lady. It's dreadful for her to have to give up her home like that. It's awful for you, too," I added, as Anna began to sniff loudly.

I put my arm round her shoulders and we walked towards the mellow, old house that would soon be no more than a memory to those who had known and loved it.

"I've never lived anywhere else and it's such a *dear* house," Anna said. "Before long it will simply be the House that Died."

"The House that Died," I repeated softly. "How sad."

John had started to help Pip clean his bike, so Anna and I left them and wandered round the beautiful flower garden at the side of *Ormond Grange*.

"Daddy still weeds it. He can't bear not to," Anna said.

"Perhaps he'll soon find a nice gardening job somewhere else," I replied, trying to sound hopeful.

"I'll have to go in soon," Anna said, when we had finished looking at the flowers, "but you'll come again tomorrow, won't you?"

"If I can. John and I came a lot when I was here before, didn't we?"

"Yes, and you must do the same now, while there's still time," Anna insisted.

Soon after that, her mother called her and she dashed away. When Pip's bike was as clean as new, he also had to go in and John and I went home. On the way I told him what Anna had said about *Ormond Grange*.

"She called it the House that Died and it sounded ever so sad. Isn't it horrid the way things don't last, not even a solid-looking house like that?"

"I reckon mansions in heaven are the only ones that last for ever," John replied, smiling.

"Mansions in heaven?" I repeated in surprise.

"Yes, I mean the ones that Jesus Christ said He would prepare for everyone who loves Him," John replied. "I... d'you know, it makes me happy to think I'll live in one of those mansions one day."

"What a cheek! How do you know you will?" I asked.

"Because that's what Jesus promised to everyone who believes that He died for them," John replied. "I haven't done anything to deserve it. He ... He's done it all for me."

"You sound a lot more religious than you used to be. I hope you won't get a mania," I said.

"No, not religious. I'm a Christian and that's quite different," John replied.

I could not see that there was any difference but did not want to argue, so I said no more. As soon as we were indoors I grabbed my case, which was still in the hall, and went upstairs.

"You're in the same room as before, dear," Aunt Nancy called after me. "So sorry, I meant to take your case up but three turkeys got out and it's been such a business catching them. Let John carry that case for you."

"It's all right, thanks," I said cheerfully, but a moment later my cheerfulness had gone.

As I entered that little bedroom I was overcome with a desolate feeling as memories of two years ago flooded back. I had been sitting on the bed in that room when Aunt Nancy appeared in the doorway holding a telegram and looking very pale and upset. She had told me as gently as she could that my mother had died. It was such a shock. She had been ill only two days.

Now, tears ran down my cheeks as I dumped my case on the floor.

"Poor Mummy. Why did it have to happen?" I whispered.

And then I remembered what John had said about the heavenly mansions that Jesus was preparing for everyone who loved Him.

"Mummy trusted in Jesus, so if it's all true perhaps she's happy now," I thought. "If only I could be sure it's true. But even if it is, that still doesn't stop me from missing Mummy so badly."

I sat on the bed again and tried to think things out, but before long I caught a glimpse of my sober face in the mirror and that made me sit up with a jerk.

"You want to be a model when you leave school," I said to myself, "but nobody's going to think much of a model with a mopy face, so you'd better cheer up a bit."

A moment later I knelt down and undid my suitcase. I pulled out my brush and comb and then stood up again and brushed my hair until it shone like silk.

"Yes," my thoughts ran on, "if only Daddy will let me go in for modelling I'll really make a name for myself, and when I'm famous lots of people will love and admire me and I'll never be lonely or unhappy."

I tried to recall when I had first made up my mind to become a model, but I could not. It almost seemed as if this ambition had always been with me, but I realised it had not. At one time I was quite happy with the idea of helping Daddy in his art and antique gallery. My new ambition must have come sometime after my last stay with Uncle Jack and Aunt Nancy.

"It ... it's almost an insecure sort of feeling," I whispered, "as if I must become famous while there's still time."

I turned with sudden energy to my case, unpacking it and putting everything away tidily. After that I went down to supper, and Uncle Jack, who had just come home, said he hoped that John and I would have a first-rate holiday together.

"Thank you, Uncle," I replied, little dreaming what that holiday held in store.

Chapter 2

MOKEY

The next day John and I went to see Pip and Anna again. Anna ran towards us and flung her thin, little arms round my waist.

"I didn't show you Mokey," she said. "Come on; let's leave the others and go to see him now."

"Who's Mokey?"

"You'll see," Anna said, dancing up and down.

It was nice to find her so much happier. Although she was three years younger than me, I had quite taken to her. Anna was lively and chatty and yet now and then there was something wistful about her that appealed to me. She led the way round the back of *Ormond Grange* and across a beautifully kept lawn to a small, green gate that opened into an old orchard.

"Come on. Race you to the other end!" Anna shouted, and off she dashed, squealing with delight when I ran after her.

"I won!" she yelled, when she reached another, larger gate, "and there's Mokey," she added, pointing into a small paddock.

"Oh, what a cute donkey!" I exclaimed.

Mokey hee-hawed with pleasure at the sound of our voices and ran towards us.

"You should have seen him when we first got him," Anna said, climbing onto the gate and fondling the donkey's long, silky ears. "He looked dreadful. His coat was all dull and there were several bare patches on his back. Daddy said it was because he hadn't been fed properly. I think he'd been starved. You could see his poor ribs sticking out."

"He looks the picture of health now, anyway," I said, stroking the donkey's soft nose.

"He's fun and he lets me ride him bare-back, don't you, Mokey?" Anna said.

She climbed higher up the gate and a moment later was proudly sitting astride the little donkey.

"Off we go," Anna said, patting him on the neck. "Show Helen how you trot."

Mokey obediently set off round the paddock. He seemed to enjoy showing off his paces.

"We guessed this is where we'd find you," a voice called, and I turned to see Pip and John approaching. "Anna can't keep away from that donkey for long. What she'll do when we've had to sell him, I hate to think," Pip said.

"Come on; you have a go," Anna shouted from the paddock.

"No thanks. I'm too big for Mokey and I'm not a bare-back rider anyway. I'm a city girl, you know, not a cowboy."

Anna was greatly tickled at the idea of my being a cowboy. She slid off the donkey and rolled in the grass, giggling. Meanwhile Mokey poked his head over the gate and hee-hawed loudly. His head moved up and down as if he was enjoying the joke as well.

"There's nothing to laugh about really," Pip said to Mokey. "Do you know, we've got to move and we've nowhere to go. Dad thinks he'll have to take you back to the market and sell you."

"No, no. He mustn't!" Anna cried, scrambling to her feet. "Suppose someone cruel bought him and he went all thin and patchy again!"

"He can't stay with us if we've nowhere to keep him," Pip said.

"There's got to be somewhere for us to live with a grassy bit for Mokey, too," Anna said, near to tears.

I told Anna not to upset herself and we all walked slowly through the orchard.

"I wonder if we'll find a new home soon," Pip said, looking unusually glum.

"I've been praying that you will," John replied, flushing slightly.

"But God doesn't answer when I ask Him for things," Anna said. "I've prayed for weeks for a new bike like Pip's but it hasn't come yet."

"Perhaps God knows you wouldn't be safe on the roads," John replied, smiling. "He's sometimes said No to me when I've asked for the wrong things, but I'm sure He won't say No this time."

"If we don't find somewhere soon and Daddy can't get a job, we'll all die of cold and hunger, won't we?" Anna asked, wide-eyed and afraid.

"But you *will* find somewhere," John said, and the calm assurance of his voice baffled me.

"He sounds so confident," I thought. "But how can he be sure? New homes don't grow like mushrooms."

Much as I hoped Pip and Anna would soon find a new home, I did not really believe praying about it would help, though I did not say so.

"Ooo, look! There's the jam factory man," Anna exclaimed, clutching my arm, "and there's another man with him."

We all peeped over the hedge and saw the two men staring up at the roof of *Ormond Grange*. Mr. Randall, or the jam factory man as Anna called him, was pointing to the gabled chimneys and talking to the other man.

"Surely they aren't pulling the Grange down yet," Pip said in dismay. "They must wait until we've found somewhere else to go."

He vaulted the small, green gate and ran towards the men, who turned as he approached them.

Chapter 3

MISS ORMOND

"Please, you aren't demolishing the house yet, are you?" we heard Pip ask. "Only we still live here. Dad can't find anywhere else to go."

Pip's freckled face was far from jolly now. He looked grave and strained as he appealed to the men.

"Don't fret, son," Mr. Randall said kindly. "Miss Ormond phoned to say she was concerned about you. Between us, we hit on a plan. I've just told Mr. Gibbs, my foreman here, to leave the lodge by the gate until last so that you can live there a while."

"Coo, thanks a lot!" Pip said.

"As I've just told your father, I want the whole site cleared this summer, so it will have to be for a few weeks only," Mr. Randall went on.

"It will help while Dad goes on searching," Pip replied.

"There's an important condition to my offer," Mr. Randall said. "You children must promise to keep away from the house, otherwise there could be a nasty accident when my men start work."

"We'll promise," Pip said, his face jolly and bright once more, "and it's super of you to think of us."

"Well, my boy, one good turn deserves another," Mr. Randall said pleasantly. "Your father has promised to keep trespassers away after my men knock off. You'd be surprised what people will help themselves to, given half a chance."

I had hardly noticed the lodge before, but now we all

ran round the front to look at it. We found Pip's parents had wasted no time. Mrs. Taylor had already flung the windows open and was busily sweeping the floor.

"No one's lived here for ages," Anna said excitedly, "but that doesn't matter. Just think, we can keep Mokey a bit longer and perhaps we won't have to sell him after all."

"Isn't Miss Ormond nice?" Pip said. "It's just like her to think of us. She asked me after church last Sunday if we were fixed yet and looked quite upset when I said we weren't."

Church! Suddenly I was disappointed with Pip. I knew John went regularly, but I had no idea Pip went, too. I wondered how often, but Anna did not give me a chance to ask.

"I've got a super idea!" she shouted, jumping up and down. "Let's take Miss Ormond some flowers after dinner. She loved her roses and the blue campanula growing in that wild bit; let's take her some of each."

We all thought it a nice gesture and I looked forward to seeing Miss Ormond again. As it turned out, only Anna and I went. Pip and John stayed behind to help Mr. and Mrs. Taylor take their carpets and other belongings to the lodge, as Mr. Randall had asked them to move at once.

It was a long walk to Oaklands Old People's Home. Anna and I passed several factories and a gasworks on the way, and the streets were jammed with traffic. At last Anna pointed to a row of trees that looked strangely out of place beside a grubby factory.

"The home's behind those trees," she said. "Miss Ormond doesn't like living there much. She says it's noisy. Her room's at the back and there's a railway at the end of the garden. She can't sleep for trucks being shunted at night."

"Perhaps she'll get used to it," I said, as we walked up the gravel drive. "Crumbs, what a dreary place after *Ormond Grange*," I added. "Aren't square, grey houses horrid? I'd hate to live here."

"Mummy says Miss Ormond's always had a lot to do with this home," Anna went on. "She used to be on the committee that runs it. She told Mummy they want to build a nicer home but they haven't enough money. They're saving up and Mummy thinks Miss Ormond's given them some money, too."

When Anna had told me that she ran up some dingy, stone steps and tugged at an old-fashioned door bell.

"Not so hard!" I exclaimed, for the bell clanged like a fire alarm.

Anna said later that the dark-haired girl who let us in was called Kathleen. She and her friend Susan helped with the housework at the home and served the old ladies with their meals.

Anna knew which was Miss Ormond's room, so she grabbed the flowers I had been carrying and scampered off. I followed her up two flights of creaky stairs and into a small bed-sitting-room.

"Why, my dearie, how thoughtful of you," I heard Miss Ormond say in a soft, gentle voice.

She was just as I remembered her, small and dainty with the whitest hair imaginable. Her face was lined and yet there was something radiant and serene about it.

"This is Helen, John's cousin," Anna said. "She came once before but it was ages ago."

"I remember you, dear," Miss Ormond said, holding out her thin, little hand in welcome.

Next she fetched a vase and we watched her arrange the flowers.

"These roses come from the bush nearest the house, I know," she said.

"They're starting to pull the house down the day after tomorrow," Anna replied sadly, "but it was nice of you to ring Mr. Randall about us."

"Well, I've prayed for you all," Miss Ormond said, "and last Sunday God put it into my heart very plainly that I should try and arrange for you to stay where you are a little longer. Don't worry, Anna dear; everything will work out all right. Our Heavenly Father knows when a sparrow falls to the ground, so be sure He knows and cares about you."

Miss Ormond, I noticed, talked with the same calm assurance as John and yet somehow I did not mind. All the same it mystified me how anyone could be so sure.

"It's almost as if they *know* God," I thought.

Altogether Miss Ormond was so kind and sincere that I knew I could trust her with even my innermost secrets.

"If I told her about the things that make me feel sad and unsafe she would understand and care, the same as she does about Anna and Pip," I thought, deciding to talk to her alone as soon as I could.

Before we left, Anna promised to bring some more flowers.

"It's a pity not to pick them, the workmen will only drop things on them," she said. "We'll bring a bigger bunch next time."

"That would be lovely," Miss Ormond replied. "Maybe Kathleen or Susan would decorate the dining room or lounge with them. I'm sure they wouldn't mind."

"I'll do it," I said eagerly, for I loved arranging flowers and wanted to please Miss Ormond.

It was past tea time when we got back to *Ormond Grange*, and John had gone home.

"I must fly, or Aunt Nancy will be cross with me," I said.

"Come again soon," Anna begged. "I couldn't bear watching the house being pulled down, on my own."

Two days later John and I went to *Ormond Grange* again. We helped Mr. and Mrs. Taylor get straight in the lodge, and two of Mr. Randall's men brought the heavy furniture in. It was as well there was plenty to do; it stopped our feeling sad about the house.

We heard several loud crashes and Anna ran out to see what caused them. She returned to tell us that a gable or chimney stack had fallen.

"The men are banging everywhere and they're enjoying it, cruel things," she said.

"Don't you go too near," Mrs. Taylor warned. "It's dangerous when old houses come down. Sometimes a whole wall collapses, so keep well away; that goes for all of you."

We repeated the promise Pip had already made to Mr. Randall, little guessing how soon we would forget it, or why.

Chapter 4

AN EXCITING DISCOVERY

That afternoon Mr. Taylor applied for a job in Barfold, and Mrs. Taylor went shopping. While they were away, we sat in the orchard watching the workmen knocking the mossy, old tiles off the roof. Had it been any other house, we would have thought it fun the way the tiles crashed down to shatter on the ground.

Suddenly one of the men shouted to his mate, who clambered over the roof to him. We saw them peer through the rafters and then look at one another in bewilderment.

"Bill, Bill, where are you?" one of them shouted.

A moment later curly-haired Bill appeared.

"What d'you want?" he growled.

"Tell Mr. Gibbs we can see a loftful of trunks and things," the man said, and Bill went, looking bored and unwilling.

"That's mighty odd!" Pip said, jumping up. "We made sure all the rooms were empty ages ago."

Soon Mr. Gibbs came along with Bill, who pointed to the two men. Mr. Gibbs joined them on the roof and peered through the rafters. We waited for him to come down and then ran forward eagerly.

"Please, what's up there?" Pip asked.

"A loftful of goodness knows what," Mr. Gibbs said.

"It must be a secret attic; what fun!" Anna squealed.

"Do you youngsters remember an attic door at the top of the house?" Mr. Gibbs asked.

"There's two, but the attics are empty," Pip said, greatly puzzled.

"We'll show you if you like," Anna offered eagerly.

"Better let the young lady find a third door, hadn't we?" the foreman said to Pip.

"Come on, Helen. Let's all search for hidden treasure," John said, with a broad grin.

We followed Anna and Mr. Gibbs into the house and up the stairs. Anna stood on a small landing at the top, looking very perplexed.

"Here's the two attics," she said.

Mr. Gibbs glanced into them, then crossed the landing to a large water tank.

"We want another door here," he said.

"But that tank's always been there," Pip said.

"Not always. Water wouldn't have been laid on until long after this house was built," Mr. Gibbs replied. "I reckon this tank hides the door to another loft. I'll get one of the chaps to shift it."

While we waited Pip and John rapped on the side of the tank.

"Hope it's empty," John said, "else we'll get drowned in the effort."

"Hurry up, Mr. Gibbs!" Pip exclaimed, pulling himself up and trying to look over the top.

"Just imagine! Mr. Gibbs said there were about twelve trunks hidden away," Anna said, turning to me. "Whatever's in them?"

"Don't get too excited or you could have a big disappointment," I said, trying to hide my own excitement.

And then the foreman returned with a workman armed with big spanners and a heavy iron bar.

"Hop it, you youngsters, while we shift the tank," Mr. Gibbs said, pushing us into an attic.

They soon disconnected the pipes and we watched

them lever the tank onto its side. Mr. Gibbs pushed it away from the recess and shone a torch up and down the wall. It was thick with dust and cobwebs but, in spite of the dirt, we all saw the same thing at once—a brass door-knob!

"There is a door!" Anna shrieked.

She jumped up and down and I had to stop her dashing across to it.

"You are mean. Don't you want to find lost, family jewels or trunks of gold?" she asked.

We all laughed and then held our ears to deafen the loud, splintering noise as the workman forced the door open. We coughed and spluttered at the cloud of dust he made. Mr. Gibbs recovered first. He went into the loft and we heard him whistle with amazement.

"Come on, one at a time, for a quick look," he invited.

Anna was through the door in a flash and we heard her squeals of delight.

"Look! A tiny rocking chair," she said, "and there's a funny, old clock, and that's a spinning wheel!"

Curiosity overcame us and we all crowded in.

"A couple of harps over there, d'you see?" Mr. Gibbs said.

"Fancy all these things being hidden away," Pip said. "Those metal boxes look interesting!"

I noticed some picture frames thickly covered with dust, but it was the trunks that interested me most. I longed to open one, but Mr. Gibbs turned us out and wedged the door shut.

"Well, well," he said, brushing the dust from his clothes, "I'll have to ask Mr. Randall what's to be done with that little lot."

We clattered downstairs, Mr. Gibbs and the workman following more slowly. We all blinked in the bright sunlight and I felt I was waking from an adventurous dream.

The foreman told his men to cover the hole in the roof with a tarpaulin and then he drove off in his van. We guessed he had gone to see Mr. Randall.

"Will Mr. Gibbs open the trunks when he gets back?" Anna asked.

"He and Mr. Randall might do it privately," Pip said.

"How mean!" Anna exclaimed.

We were still talking when the foreman returned.

"Mr. Randall's out but I've left a message," he said. "Now, off you go; there's work to be done."

"When Daddy comes home I'll ask *him* to open the trunks," Anna said.

"But he can't, silly; *Ormond Grange* is nothing to do with us now," Pip reminded her.

"Oh, but it is!" Anna argued, near to tears of exasperation.

Chapter 5

WE LEND A HAND

The next morning John and I went early to *Ormond Grange*, but the workmen were already there. They were busy demolishing the west wing of the house and Pip and Anna were watching them from a safe distance. We had scarcely joined them when Mr. Gibbs arrived in his little van.

"I've news for you youngsters. Mr. Randall's told me the things in the loft are to be treated as Miss Ormond's and he wants the old lady to have a look at them," he said. "She's willing if there's anything worth looking at," he added.

"Of course everything's Miss Ormond's. It's her house," Anna replied.

"It was," Pip corrected her.

"Look here, if your mum and dad don't object, and you wear your oldest clothes, how would you like to help bring some of the smaller things down into the hall?" Mr. Gibbs asked next.

"Wouldn't we just!" Pip exclaimed, and I was glad I was wearing my shabbiest jeans, as I was keen to help, too.

The foreman assured Mrs. Taylor that the staircase was still quite safe, so she gave her permission for us to enter the house. It was only then that we remembered we had broken our previous promise, but Mrs. Taylor excused us as Mr. Gibbs had been with us and we had gone into the house for a special reason.

We lost no time in climbing up to the loft once more and Mr. Gibbs opened the door for us.

"My men will be taking the heavy stuff downstairs," he told us, "but you youngsters can take the smaller bits and pieces."

Anna made a dive for the spinning wheel and I picked up the little rocking chair and a copper warming pan. Pip and John carried down several gilt-framed paintings between them. They were very old and dirty so none of us bothered to look at them. We made several trips up and down before anyone else came to help, but at last four workmen appeared. They brought all the trunks down, grumbling the whole time about its not really being their job.

It took all the morning to clear the loft, and by then the hall of *Ormond Grange* looked like a left luggage office, except that the luggage had obviously been left for an unusually long time.

Anna darted all over the place and tended to get in the way, so I sent her off for a pencil and paper. When she came back she helped me to make a list of some of the things in the hall, a pair of bellows, an enormous, black kettle and a family Bible among them. I opened the Bible and was surprised to see that it contained an Ormond family tree on the first page. The tree went back to the seventeenth century, but the latest name added to it was Alicia Emma Ormond, born 8th November, 1890.

Anna was very interested in the Bible and asked me to read the beautiful, copperplate writing on the page next to the family tree. Although the page was yellow with age and the ink faded, I could just make out the words.

"Unto God, Who is able to do exceeding abundantly above all that we ask or think," I read out loud.

"That must be the family motto," Anna said.

"Pardon me, but it's a verse from the Bible," John corrected, smiling at her.

He looked over my shoulder and read the words for himself.

"I wonder how many Ormonds proved those words true in their own lives," he said.

I shut the old Bible without answering, but it was odd how I could not forget those words. I did not want to remember them, yet somehow they embedded themselves in my mind. I even dreamed about them that night. They kept writing and rewriting themselves on the bedroom ceiling in the same lovely, old, copperplate lettering.

It was strange that I should have dreamed about those words and not about the contents of one of the trunks, for that interested me far more. It was only at our earnest begging that Mr. Gibbs agreed to open the trunk at all. Anna sat on the one she specially wanted to see inside and announced that she would not get off until it was opened. Mr. Gibbs weakened and, with the help of a hammer and a metal spike, he broke open the fastenings and slowly lifted the lid, while we crowded round him.

I gasped with astonishment. Inside the trunk was a beautiful, silk dress carefully packed in layers of tissue paper. It was a delicate shade of lavender and exquisitely made. I did not see all of it because the foreman flatly refused to lift it out, but I had seen enough to make me want that dress. I felt that I would have given anything to be able to wear it and show it off. Mr. Gibbs brought me back to reality by shutting the lid down and telling long-haired Bill to tie the trunk up securely with a good, stout rope.

"May I go and tell Miss Ormond about these trunks?" I asked eagerly.

I had been wanting to see Miss Ormond, anyway, and

this was an added reason for wanting to go, but Mr. Gibbs disappointed me.

"Mr. Randall's already told her, lass," he said.

"I mean tell her that they are worth looking at. Mr. Randall doesn't know that," I insisted.

Unfortunately for me, the foreman thought he had a better plan. He said that he would go to Oaklands Old People's Home himself and fetch Miss Ormond, if she were willing to travel in his van.

"The sooner the lady sees everything the better," he explained. "It's holding up my work to have this lot lying around. She'll have to say what she wants done with it."

That afternoon Miss Ormond did come to the Grange in the foreman's van and we ran to her eagerly, all talking at once. She was astonished to find how many reminders of the past awaited her view. At first she seemed too bewildered to know what to do, but suddenly she had an idea.

"I know; I'll call in my old friend Mr. Tomkinson. He's the museum curator, and he'll advise me what to keep," she said. "I'm afraid I don't feel equal to examining all those trunks myself."

Miss Ormond then wanted to know exactly how we had discovered the loft so we told her about the door behind the water tank.

"How extraordinary! That tank's been there as long as I can remember," she said. "Wait a minute, though. The house was taken over by the Army in the First World War and used as an officer's billet. Maybe the tank was put in then. The Army wouldn't have bothered about covering the entrance to a cluttered, old loft."

Mr. Tomkinson was a small, fussy, little man with a habit of rubbing his hands together in a quick, jerky way. He came the next day and began his examination by looking in the trunk that Mr. Gibbs had already opened. When he saw the dress he sent Anna running to her mother for an old sheet or curtain. She soon came back with a torn sheet, which Mr. Tomkinson spread on the floor. Next he carefully lifted out the dress and arranged it on the sheet with quick, fussy movements. He got into quite a state about the perfect workmanship and the spotless condition of the dress.

As I gazed at it I longed to put it on, although I could see it was too big for me.

"How old is it, and who would have worn a dress like that?" I asked.

"It's about seventy years old," Mr. Tomkinson told me, "and definitely late Victorian. The exceptionally full skirt, small waist and huge, puffed sleeves date it at around the middle eighteen nineties. It's an excellent example of a young lady's ball gown, an excellent example. Not unique, of course, not unique but remarkably well preserved."

"There's some more things at the bottom of the trunk," Anna said, nearly tipping in head first in her eagerness.

We all laughed when Mr. Tomkinson pulled out an old-fashioned, whalebone corset, complete with lacings; then he showed us four swirling petticoats to be worn with the lavender dress.

"Dear me, what a pity," Mr. Tomkinson said, as he opened the next trunk. He picked up the red tunic of a military uniform but it fell to pieces in his hands

"Moths have been breeding in here for years," he said, then he lifted out a long, ceremonial sword in a heavily ornamented sheath. He tried to withdraw it but it was too badly rusted to move.

After opening several other trunks and finding them full of clothes, the curator turned to Mr. Gibbs.

"I must ask Miss Ormond's permission to remove

these," he said. "It will be much easier to inspect everything properly in my own store rooms, yes, much easier, and it will get them out of your way."

Mr. Gibbs was obviously relieved by this suggestion and we heard later that Miss Ormond gladly gave her consent for the trunks to be taken to the museum. In fact she was almost as excited as Anna and I when Mr. Tomkinson told her he would like to make a special display of the beautiful, lavender dress and other interesting items. The only frustration for all of us was the curator's warning that it would take several days to get the discoveries listed and sorted.

"Several days, oh yes, it's sure to take several days," Anna said, imitating Mr. Tomkinson's quick, nervous manner, and we could not help laughing in spite of our disappointment.

John told me how carefully the curator had handled the dirty, old pictures that did not seem to be worth anything, and we both agreed how fortunate Miss Ormond was that he should be there to take charge.

"I do wish Daddy wasn't searching for antiques in Italy right now," I said. "He'd be thrilled to know we've discovered some right here in England. He's always hoped I'd follow in his footsteps and go in for antiques and art."

"And will you?" John asked.

"Not really. I'm going to be ... something quite different," I stammered.

On the spur of the moment I had almost let it out that I had set my heart on becoming a famous fashion model, but John was the last person to blurt that out to.

Chapter 6

MORE ABOUT THE TRUNKS

Two days passed without any further news of the trunks. On the third day Anna could bear it no longer, but then she had a good idea.

"We promised to take some more flowers to Oaklands and we forgot all about it," she said to me. "Let's take some today and we can ask Miss Ormond if she's heard anything more at the same time."

"You scheming, little monkey. Helen shouldn't encourage you," Pip said, a broad grin on his freckled face.

But I wanted to see Miss Ormond again, so I willingly fell in with Anna's suggestion and helped her pick a large bunch of flowers. This time it was Susan who answered the door to us. She was as fair as Kathleen was dark and she smiled pleasantly when she saw the flowers.

"How kind of you. Hardly anyone brings us flowers, specially straight from a garden," she said. "They smell marvellous and the old ladies will love them."

Susan accepted my offer to help arrange the flowers and led the way to the kitchen, where the vases were kept.

"Why, hello," said Kathleen, who was busy in the kitchen. "You've come on a good day. Miss Ormond was only saying this morning that she's got some news for you. It's about those trunks the workmen discovered at *Ormond Grange*. Wasn't it exciting? I wish I'd been there."

I wanted to dash up to Miss Ormond's room straight away but could hardly leave the flowers. I arranged them as quickly as I could, while Anna chattered to Kathleen and Susan about the spinning wheel, the harps and the old, family Bible.

"Tell us what you know," I said to Kathleen, when I could get a word in.

"Not much, but Mr. Tomkinson called yesterday evening and Miss Ormond hinted that something special's being planned as a result. She also hinted that Susan and I might like to help."

"I know, a mannequin parade to display some lovely, old dresses!" I exclaimed. "Oh, I simply must see Miss Ormond!"

"Why, are you keen on that sort of thing?" Kathleen asked.

"I should say I am. I intend to be a fashion model one day and I adore anything to do with clothes. If you don't mind, I think I'll go and see . . ."

A ring at the door checked my words and Susan hurried off to answer it. Some time passed before she returned. When she did she was quite excited.

"That was Mr. Tomkinson again, and he's taken up some gorgeous dresses, to show Miss Ormond," she said.

That news was as good as an invitation to Anna and me. We rushed upstairs as fast as we could go, only checking ourselves to knock on the door before entering Miss Ormond's room. She was pleased to see us and obviously did not think we were intruding.

"Poor Mr. Tomkinson, he's been so busy," she said. "He's even had a reporter from a local paper along, hoping to make front page news of the discoveries at the Grange."

I only half listened to what she was saying because I was entranced by the sight of the lovely gowns spread round the room, but Anna clapped her hands with glee.

"We helped to find them! We're famous," she said. "Can we have our pictures in the paper?"

"I'm afraid the reporter must wait until we're ready to make everything public," Miss Ormond replied gently.

She then asked the curator to tell us the latest news from the museum.

"First of all I must say what a pleasure it has been to deal with such an excellent collection of Victorian and Edwardian costumes," Mr. Tomkinson said, rubbing his hands together. "Someone must have put them away with great care, yes, with great care."

"That would have been my mother," Miss Ormond told him. "She always put things away carefully, saying you could never tell when they would come in useful again."

"Thanks to Mrs. Ormond, we've got some examples of period styles that could be worn today," Mr. Tomkinson said. "In those days the craftsman's touch was on everything and those trunks have kept the years out remarkably well. It's a pity they didn't all keep the moths out, a great pity. The little wretches have ruined a blue riding habit and a fur-trimmed velvet cloak."

I went over to Miss Ormond's bed to admire a dainty, white, child's dress lying there.

"Is this seventy years old?" I asked. "The material doesn't look old at all."

"It's surprising how some materials last, most surprising," Mr. Tomkinson said. "Actually we've got examples in the museum of clothes that were worn two hundred years ago. They have to be handled with great care, of course, but these are quite modern by comparison, quite modern."

He went on to tell Miss Ormond that there was not enough room at the museum to display everything found at *Ormond Grange,* which was why he had suggested a special show should be put on at the Old People's Home.

"You told me yesterday that you will soon be holding a fête to help with your Rebuilding Fund, so what could be better than combining a special display with the fête? It should prove a great attraction, don't you think? A great attraction."

"I mentioned your suggestion to two members of the committee this morning and they were most enthusiastic," Miss Ormond replied, "so I do hope you will go ahead and arrange it. It is most kind of you to take the trouble."

"Can I help, too?" Anna asked.

"I believe you can," Mr. Tomkinson said. "You see, we want to make the display as interesting as we can. I therefore plan to have a few girls modelling some of the gowns, yes, modelling them. Would you like to take part?"

"Yes please! Can I wear that white dress on the bed?" Anna asked.

"If it will fit you, and I believe it will," Mr. Tomkinson said.

"I'm sure Kathleen and Susan would like to help as well," Miss Ormond said.

"So would I!" I exclaimed, and all at once I began to tremble with excitement.

Perhaps I could wear something as elegant as the gown we had first seen. That one was too big, I knew, but surely there would be something else, just right for me. Then, as Anna had said, I would get my picture in the paper—maybe even in a woman's glossy magazine. Imagine my name appearing in print! What a wonderful first step towards becoming a world-famous model!

These were the thoughts that went racing through my head and for days after, so that I could think of nothing else but the coming display.

"There'll be something absolutely gorgeous just right for me!" I kept telling myself over and over again.

At last Miss Ormond sent Anna and me a message, asking us to come to Oaklands again as Mr. Tomkinson was bringing some more clothes from the trunks. I was so thrilled that I hardly ate any lunch that day. I did so hope that 'my' dress would be the loveliest of all.

At first I had wanted to see Miss Ormond again only to pour out my troubles. Now I was so thrilled about the fashion display that I quite forgot my reason for wanting to see her!

Chapter 7

THE TRY ON

Anna and I arrived at Oaklands long before Mr. Tomkinson was due, and we waited impatiently. At last his van appeared in the drive and we saw that he had brought a lady assistant with him. We also saw that the back of his van was filled with gowns of all colours.

"Crumbs, we can't wear all those! There's only four of us, counting Kathleen and Susan," Anna said.

"I've brought all the clothes that can safely be worn," Mr. Tomkinson told us. "Safely for the clothes, that is, not necessarily safely for the wearers."

I was greatly intrigued to hear that but before I could ask him what he meant Susan and Kathleen joined us. He told them that he would like them to select styles from different periods as he wanted the general effect to be one of contrast.

Mr. Tomkinson and his assistant took the dresses and gowns to a spare room where we could change, and then he turned to me.

"You're Helen, aren't you?"

I felt my face flush and wondered breathlessly why he had singled me out.

"We have only one dress suitable for you, only one," Mr. Tomkinson went on in his fussy way. "You are an in-between size, I fear, and adult clothes would not fit."

My heart thumped wildly. Would it be exactly the sort of dress I wanted to wear?—something like the one I had seen at *Ormond Grange.*

"Jean dear, will you bring Helen's costume next?" Mr. Tomkinson called to his assistant, who was on the way downstairs again. I waited on the landing for her to come back. To my horror, she brought with her a sombre-looking outfit made of maroon poplin. It was awful! Feeling sick with disappointment, I followed her into the changing room.

"It's quite nice, don't you think?" Jean asked, showing me the dreary dress and matching jacket, also a pair of button-sided boots. "It's a young lady's walking costume. Slip the jacket on."

I put my arms unwillingly into the sleeves and tried to pull the jacket on, but it was too small and dragged tightly across my shoulders.

"It's too tight; what a shame," Jean said, not noticing the relief my face must have shown.

I felt I would have run to the end of the earth rather than be seen wearing a thing like that. I pulled it off in disgust, and Jean left me standing there while she turned her attention to Susan and Kathleen.

"You won't put anything on that can't be fastened easily, will you?" she said. "We don't want anything split."

She went on to explain that many of the styles were made to be worn by extremely slim, young ladies.

"They really did have wasp waists in those days, I can tell you," she said. "Not to worry, though; if either of you need to lose a few inches we have the very thing here—whalebone corsets. I'm an expert at tight lacing, so all's well."

Only Kathleen seemed to notice my bitter disappointment. All at once I felt I had to get away from Oaklands and the tantalising dresses that did not fit me. I dived for the door and Kathleen caught hold of my arm as I passed.

"Hard luck, Helen," she whispered, "but don't fret. You'll get your turn in the limelight one day."

I was too choked to answer and ran down the stairs and out of the house before anyone else could stop me. It was mean to dash off like that without Anna, but I could not face her excited chatter all the way home. I was so sick with disappointment that all I wanted to do was to get away and be entirely on my own for a while.

My footsteps took me back to *Ormond Grange* almost automatically and I didn't notice a thing on the way, but noisy demolition work was in full swing at the Grange, so I avoided the house and went down to the paddock.

Mokey, the little donkey, came to the gate when he saw me, but he was not the bright, little creature who usually came to greet any of us. His ears flopped dismally and when he hee-hawed that sounded dismal, too. He put his head over the gate and nuzzled my hand dejectedly.

"Whatever's the matter, Mokey?" I asked. "You look just about as fed up as I feel. Is it because *Ormond Grange* is being pulled down? Do you know that you may yet have to be sold and say good-bye to your paddock for ever?"

I stayed a long time by that gate, idly fondling the donkey's drooping ears. As I stood there my thoughts turned inwards to my own bitter disappointment.

"Do you know, Mokey? I'm the only one out of four girls who wants to be a model—the only one who cares about displaying dresses, and yet I'm the only one who can't take part in showing off the fashions of long ago. Don't you think it's unfair?"

The little donkey hee-hawed again and nodded his head up and down over the top of the gate.

"I'm glad you agree with me," I said, "but I will be a success one day, you see if I'm not."

Chapter 8

ANNA TURNS THE TABLES ON ME

After a while, an empty feeling made me realise how little lunch I had eaten and how near to tea time it must be. I left the paddock and hurried down the road. I had not gone far when I saw John and Anna coming towards me.

"Where have you been?" Anna demanded, darting forward. "We looked everywhere for you."

"I . . . er, well there was nothing for me to wear so I got out of the way," I replied. "I've been to see Mokey. He looked lonely."

"But you shouldn't have left Anna to come home alone. Wasn't there something you could do to help the others?" John remonstrated.

"What made you turn up at Oaklands, anyway?" I countered.

"Pip's gone to Barfold with his parents. His Dad thinks he's got a job there so they've gone to look for somewhere to live. Poor old Pip's pretty blue about it. Anyway, in the meantime I went to see if I could help with arranging the fête. Lucky I did; otherwise, Anna would have had to cross the busy roads on her own."

"I wouldn't have minded," Anna said quickly. "Poor Helen! Kathleen told me there was nothing for you to wear. I wish you had seen me in my dress, though. Everyone said how pretty I looked. It's a full-skirted party dress with a wide, satin sash that ties in a big bow. I also wore frilly pantaloons and they were so long that the lace frills showed below the dress."

"Yes, I saw the things you're wearing, the other day," I replied.

John and I left Anna at the lodge and went home. John was not interested in the dress display, but he was enthusiastic about the fête generally.

"I'm sure we'll have a good crowd to it," he said. "It's being given lots of publicity, so we should raise plenty of money for the Rebuilding Fund. Unfortunately, the chairman of Oaklands Committee can't open the fête because he's away on business. They've got to find someone else to do it."

"I can't see how they'll ever raise enough money to build another Old People's Home, just by holding fêtes and things," I said.

"Nor me; Pip said even the smallest house costs a fortune. That's why the Taylors can't afford a place of their own. But still we must all do what we can. Every bit of help brings the goal nearer, doesn't it? And Oaklands is pretty gloomy. I'd hate to live there."

"Me, too," I agreed.

"That reminds me, I've offered to run a stall on fête day. Will you help me?"

I still wanted to take part in the dress display but helping John run a stall would be better than doing nothing. I was glad he had asked me because we had not spent much time together on this holiday. He had been on several cycling outings with Pip, planning them specially to stop Pip worrying too much about having to move.

I did not agree with John over lots of things but he was very steady and reliable and I enjoyed working with him. One day when we had stopped for a breather Kathleen brought us a cup of tea. She stayed to tell me I was not the only one who had been disappointed over the dress display. She said she had wanted to wear the lovely, lavender ball gown we all admired, but she was not tall enough. Susan would be wearing that, even though it would mean lacing up her waist very tightly.

John lost interest in the conversation as Kathleen went on to say she would be wearing something entirely different. She did not want to, but she was trying it on when Mr. Tomkinson had called her and Susan downstairs.

"Susan swept down grandly, the yards and yards of frills and flounces in her skirt showing off her tiny waist a treat," Kathleen said enviously, "but I wasn't so lucky, having just wriggled into a long, narrow skirt. Mr. Tomkinson seemed delighted that I was wearing something so different from Susan. It was the sort of contrast he wanted."

Kathleen had then told Mr. Tomkinson she did not like the skirt and was afraid she might split the seams or tear the hem, but the curator had merely looked up his list and quoted 'skirt with reinforced side seams and hem finished off with heavy brading'

"It's not the costume we need to worry about," he had said. "No, not the costume, only the person inside it."

When Kathleen said that, I understood what the curator had meant when he spoke about safety of the costumes not safety of the wearers. Anyway, when Mr. Tomkinson's assistant had brought the jacket and found it fitted Kathleen perfectly, she had finally agreed to display it.

"Honestly, the things I do for Oaklands," Kathleen said, "but still, I've only got to wear the thing for an hour or two."

That same day Miss Ormond told me Mr. Randall had called the previous evening and had been so interested in the things from *Ormond Grange* that he had stayed quite a while. Before he left he had agreed to open the fête and even promised to send some preserves from his factory as a gift for one of the stalls.

Miss Ormond's voice quavered as she told us of the quantity of jam and marmalade that had already been delivered. The word 'jam' was a cruel reminder that her lovely, old home was being pulled down and that a factory would soon stand in its place.

As the fête drew nearer, Anna and Pip came to help and we were glad they did. We all worked hard in the garden, setting up stalls and later helping to decorate the large hall and dining-room where the dress display and exhibition of antiques were to be held.

On the afternoon before the fête, Mr. Tomkinson arrived with a van full of exhibits. He fussed about a great deal, moving tables and tut-tutting because everything was not arranged exactly as he wanted. It took so long to get the hall right and to unpack his exhibits that I did not notice Anna had disappeared. It was not until Pip asked me where she was that I realised I had not seen her for ages.

Pip was hot and flustered with all the lifting and carrying he had done and suggested irritably that she must be hiding. I searched everywhere but there was still no sign of Anna.

"Perhaps she went back to *Ormond Grange* alone," I said.

"She shouldn't have done. She knows Mum doesn't like her crossing busy roads by herself."

"She may have gone to talk to Mokey. I told her the other day that he was lonely."

"I'd better go and make sure she's all right," Pip said.

"Let me go," I offered, since Pip was so busy.

He agreed willingly, so I set off at once for *Ormond Grange*. But Anna was nowhere about and the lodge was deserted. I ran to the paddock but she was not there, either. Suddenly my anxiety doubled. The paddock gate was open and Mokey had gone. Then I saw Anna's straw hat lying in the grass. It was the one she had worn to Oaklands that afternoon.

"So she *has* been here," I said. "Whatever's happened?"

Chapter 9

MOKEY AGAIN

I ran back to the road, worrying over what could have happened. All at once I recalled what John had said about the Taylors moving to Barfold.

"Anna must have run away with Mokey rather than have him sold," I said aloud.

The more I thought about it, the more likely it seemed that I was right. The only thing to do was to find Anna and bring her back.

Leaving *Ormond Grange* I took the road up the hill to the left. The road to the right led into town and it was unlikely that Anna and Mokey would have gone that way.

I hurried as fast as I could, but going uphill made me out of breath and I had to stop for a breather at the crossroads at the top. Each road seemed to lead through woods and there was no way of telling which one Anna would have taken. There were only a few houses here, large ones standing in their own grounds, and there was no one around who might have seen a small girl and a donkey.

Suddenly I saw something which filled me with hope. In the soft earth beside one road were small hoof marks! I set off again, half running and half walking. I got hotter and hotter and more and more out of breath but did not catch sight of Anna and Mokey.

"I'll never find them on my own," I panted at last. "They couldn't have got this far."

I turned back wearily, wondering what John and Pip would have to say when I told them that Anna was lost. But, as I rounded a bend in the road, there she was in front of me, leading Mokey through the gateway of a large house!

"Anna!" I yelled.

She turned and waved delightedly. Before I could scold her, she told me how bored she had become with everyone so busy at Oaklands. She had decided to go and see Mokey, who had snatched her hat and run round the paddock. When she opened the gate to catch him, Mokey had promptly galloped through, dropping her hat as he went.

"He was very naughty," Anna went on. "He wouldn't stop when I called and I had to run up the road after him. Twice I nearly caught him but then he ran faster. Where do you think he stopped in the end?"

"In the garden of that big house, by the look of it."

"Yes, but you'll never guess who owns it!" Anna said excitedly. "It's Mr. Randall's."

"Crumbs! Was he there?"

"Yes, snoozing in a deck chair. You should have seen him jump when Mokey trotted up and nuzzled him on the shoulder. But he laughed when he saw it was only a donkey. I told him what had happened and he was ever so nice. I also told him we'd got to move to Barfold and how awful it would be for Mokey."

"Oh, Anna, you shouldn't have done that!"

"Well, I did. I begged him to leave the paddock for Mokey, but he said he was building tennis courts there. Isn't it a shame? Still, he did say Daddy was to let him know when we move. He thinks he knows a farmer who might take Mokey."

"Really? That's wonderful," I said.

"You clever, little donkey," Anna exclaimed, flinging

her arms round his neck. "Perhaps you've found yourself a nice new home after all."

Then suddenly she looked very sad.

"If only we hadn't got to go," she said. "I'll lose all my school friends and never see Mokey again."

"But you'll make new friends, and at least you'll know Mokey's happy," I replied.

Anna still looked glum and I almost hoped Mr. Taylor would not get the job in Barfold after all but would find a job and a home not so far away.

After listening to Anna's adventures I had not the heart to tell her what a fright she had given me. Instead, I walked back to the crossroads, thinking how odd it was that, of all the smart residences dotted among the woods, Mokey should have picked Mr. Randall's to trespass in.

Next morning, on the very day of the fête, Miss Ormond told us that Mr. Randall had made a staggering offer to the Oaklands Committee, and I was sure Mokey was responsible. Mr. Randall had said that, if they could build a new Old People's Home on the site of *Ormond Grange*, he would be happy to swop and build his factory on the Oaklands ground!

"Indeed," Miss Ormond went on, "he was keen on the idea. He said this site would suit him much better, being nearer the railway and main road. He also added that perhaps *we* could leave the paddock for a certain young lady's donkey to live in!"

It took some moments for the full significance of Miss Ormond's words to sink in, but I recovered from my astonishment first.

"It . . . it's unbelievable," I stammered. "Just think, the money he must have spent on having *Ormond Grange* pulled down! And he's willing to spend that much all over again on Oaklands!"

"Yes, he's a wonderfully generous man," Miss Ormond

replied. "It almost breaks my heart to think we may have to turn his offer down. You see, he said he could give us only a month to decide and the committee haven't anything like enough money for the new home yet."

"Money! It's a perfect nuisance! You can't do a thing without it," I exclaimed.

Miss Ormond smiled at my outburst.

"We can pray, believing that God's power is not limited by human means," she said. "And I do believe that, if it is His will, then this place will be rebuilt on the site of my old home. I've prayed often that I might see this home rebuilt. I can't tell you how happy I'd be if this is my Heavenly Father's answer—a new home on the site of my beloved Grange!"

Miss Ormond clasped her hands together longingly and at that moment I wished I was a millionaire. I would gladly have spent a fortune to grant her wishes.

But as it was, I was full of doubts. How could her dream come true without the money to pay for a big, new building? I was quite sure even God could not answer prayers like that.

Suddenly the words in the front of the old, family Bible flashed vividly across my mind. "Unto God, Who is able to do exceeding abundantly above all that we ask or think."

"Could it be true? Could it possibly?" I wondered, with a strange feeling of awe.

Chapter 10

THE FÊTE AND AFTER

At last our preparations were finished and the day of the fête and special exhibition arrived. Although I was still disappointed at not taking part in the dress display, I could not help being thrilled when I saw Susan. She stood near the main entrance of Oaklands, looking like a beauty from Victorian times brought back to life.

"You look simply gorgeous," I said, gazing in admiration at her exquisite lavender gown.

Yet, even as I looked at that dress, I realised that it was not really the sort of thing I would have chosen to wear myself after all. It was beautiful but rather too ornate for my liking.

"I may look gorgeous, but I'd much rather be dressed in my own clothes than laced up so tightly," Susan replied. "Look at my waist! It's pulled in to twenty-one inches and I can hardly breathe."

"Let me see your lovely fan," I said, to help her think of something else.

Susan held it out and I saw that it was carved of many pieces of ivory opening out to form a lovely pattern, almost as if it were worked in lace.

"There are some more like it in the exhibition," Susan told me.

"Let's look round together and..." I began, but she interrupted me.

"Don't be silly, I mustn't move around in this dress,"

she said. "The skirt sticks out so far that I'd knock things over. And just look at my sleeves!"

I had not specially noticed them before, but now I saw that from the shoulder to the elbow they were padded out to an enormous size. They were skilfully embroidered and decorated with lace and satin bows but decidedly cumbersome.

"Goodness, they're nearly as big as pillows," I said. Then I hurried off for a quick preview of the exhibition on my own.

"Ask Kathleen to show you round. She'd be delighted," Susan called after me, with a mischievous grin.

I found the array of fans and marvelled at the time and patience that must have gone into creating them. Some were made of silk, folding up and slipping into elegant cases. The nicest one had blades partly covered in mother-of-pearl and finished in silk, showing the delicate hues of all the colours of the rainbow. I had just finished admiring the fans when Anna ran to me.

"Come and see Kathleen," she said, grabbing my hand.

She led the way to the large dining-room, which was now cleared of tables and chairs. We met Kathleen by the door and Anna burst into fits of giggles. She put her hands behind her back and went stalking across the room with long strides, turning and looking at us every few paces.

"Whatever's the matter with her?" I asked Kathleen.

"Don't take any notice. She's making fun of me, that's all," she replied, glancing down at her costume.

I stepped back and looked her up and down. She was wearing a two-piece suit made of an expensive-looking, dark grey material. The jacket fitted perfectly and was fastened with a row of self-covered buttons right down her left side. Her skirt was long and straight and the line of buttons continued to the hem. The whole costume had a simple, classic air that appealed to me immensely. What a contrast after Susan's gown! This one was as smooth and uncluttered as hers was fussy and over-ornate. Kathleen told me it was all the rage in 1911, whereas Susan's would have been 'the thing' in 1895.

"It's very smart. I wish I could have worn it," I said.

"Pity you couldn't. You've probably got the right sort of walk for it," Kathleen replied. "I'm anything but mannequin-minded!"

"But it suits you down to the ground," I assured her.

She smiled at my unintentional joke, but the smile quickly faded and she looked almost sorry for herself.

"Don't tease. I've had more than enough already," she said.

"I'm not. I came to ask you to show me round. Susan said..."

"Susan! She would," Kathleen broke in. "Just because I told her she looked like an egg-timer in that whalebone corset, she's been trying to get people to walk round the exhibition with me."

"What's wrong with that?" I asked.

Anna came up as if in answer to my question. She caught hold of Kathleen's hand and tried to pull her along.

"Come on. Run, run, run!" she said, but Kathleen quickly freed herself.

"Anna sees that I can hardly walk, even if you don't. I can only manage a stride of a few inches in this get-up. It's a hobble skirt, you know."

I had never heard of such a thing but did not want to admit it to Kathleen, especially as she knew I was interested in fashion and modelling. But my curiosity was aroused and I would not rest until I had found out all I could about hobble skirts, who wore them, and why.

The fête was about to begin so there was no time to look at the special exhibition after all. That would have to wait until later. I dashed off to my place beside John at the preserve stall just as the secretary of Oaklands Committee began a short speech to remind everyone that the fête was in aid of the Rebuilding Fund. He also introduced Mr. Randall and thanked Miss Ormond for so kindly allowing the dress and antique display. He said he hoped that this extra attraction would be a means of adding substantially to the fund. John and I, knowing what was at stake, hoped so, too.

When Mr. Randall came forward he made no reference to his generous offer. He merely smiled round at everybody and declared the fête open, after which the visitors turned to the various amusements and stalls. Mr. Randall was one of the first to visit John's stall, where he bought a jar of his own factory's jam!

"If only we knew where this jam was going to be made in future!" I thought, as I served him.

The fête was crowded and we were soon surrounded with customers. I felt pretty tired when at last it was all over, but when I saw Kathleen and Susan again they declared they were utterly exhausted.

"I feel as if I'll never breathe deeply again," Susan complained, fanning herself with the ivory fan.

"Never mind, it's only been for one afternoon," John said, "and the fête's been a howling success. Every stall's practically sold out. We must have raised hundreds of pounds for the fund."

"Good job, too," Kathleen said, "but I'll tell you something. It isn't only one afternoon for us. By special request, the display is going to be shown again next Wednesday. On the morning of the same day we've been asked to wear these clothes at a mannequin parade, as well."

"Not a real mannequin parade?" I asked, with a keen stab of envy.

"Yes, it's being held at Kennedy's, that's the main store in the High Street," Kathleen told me. "Only Anna's keen to go, but Miss Ormond asked us so nicely that Susan and I agreed as well. The thing is, it means more publicity for Oaklands and possibly a donation from the store. How I'm going to get along the cat-walk, hobbled like this, I hate to think."

"What's a cat-walk, anyway?" John asked.

"The raised dais that mannequins walk on," I told him.

Soon after that, Susan and Kathleen went upstairs to change into their ordinary clothes. I was going to ask John to look at some of the *Ormond Grange* exhibits with me but he, too, went upstairs to wait for Kathleen to re-appear. He told me he had something important to say to her about the parade at Kennedy's.

"That parade, what a mix-up it is!" I thought in disgust. "Kathleen and Susan aren't a bit keen to be in it and yet I'd give anything for the chance. It could have been the start of my modelling career."

And with these thoughts still uppermost in my mind I wandered off to look round the exhibition.

Chapter 11

A GLIMPSE AT THE PAST

Gradually the atmosphere of the exhibition took a hold on me until I was quite fascinated by it. Maybe it was seeing Susan and Kathleen dressed in clothes of those times that brought it home to me that they had actually been worn by real people just like us. I gazed at two figures in Victorian dresses, sitting at the harps I had first seen in the loft, and could imagine them gracefully plucking at the strings. It would have been exactly in keeping with the elegant styles of that period.

Near the harps I saw an enormous camera on a clumsy-looking tripod. Some photographs, perhaps taken with that very camera, were displayed on a table nearby. The 'latest' photographs were of quaint, old cars owned, I supposed, by the Ormond family at one time. Some of the other photographs were over a hundred years old and that surprised me. I did not know they could take photographs so long ago.

I passed on to a glass dome standing on a small table. The dome covered a host of small, stuffed birds of every hue. They were so colourful that I was sure they were not British birds. Next to the dome stood a solitary songbird in a gilded cage. While I was looking at it, Mr. Tomkinson came along specially to show another gentleman how to wind up the mechanism in the base of the cage. The bird immediately began to sing.

"How incredible that it should still be in perfect working order," the other man said. "Don't forget, if Miss Ormond wants a customer for it, here I am."

They walked away again, still talking, but I very much hoped that Miss Ormond would not part with such a treasure. I passed a small wooden cradle with a china doll in it and the little spinning wheel that Anna had liked so much, and came to a display set out like a Victorian drawing-room. Two more figures were in visiting dresses dating from the 1870s. The dresses were made of velvet. They dipped to the ground in front but were swept up high at the back and gathered into a bustle. Both figures were standing and I wondered if the ladies who wore such dresses were ever able to do anything else. A third figure was in the attitude of leaving the room, with a cloak about to be slipped over a ball gown with enormous padded sleeves like the one Susan had been wearing.

As I wandered on round the show I wished that Daddy was with me. He would have loved the bird that was still singing in its cage. He would also have been interested in a little writing desk with a top made up of differently coloured pieces of wood all set together in an intricate pattern. Nearby was an old chessboard complete with a set of ebony and ivory chessmen. Behind them stood a row of old books, one of which was a specially bound copy of *The Pilgrim's Progress*.

"The things they found in that loft!" I exclaimed.

Before long I found myself standing near Mr. Tomkinson and his companion again. The curator was pointing out some paintings that had been specially cleaned, or 'restored' as he put it, by his museum staff. Others were shown in an uncleaned state and I was astonished at the difference; they were drab and lifeless by comparison.

"There were several paintings in the attic," Mr. Tomkinson was saying. "Some I shan't have touched until an expert has examined them."

I wanted to butt in and beg him to let Daddy do the examining, but of course I couldn't. It would have been an awful cheek. As I walked on I wondered what would happen to everything when the display was over. Mr. Tomkinson had already said that his museum could not house it all.

Next I came to the display that fascinated me most. It was a collection of costumes fitted onto a group of tailor's dummies. Each one bore a card showing the name of the style and the period from which it came. There was an 1850 crinoline in the middle, and again it puzzled me how women moved about or sat down dressed like that. Nearby was a dress with a skirt drawn up into a bustle at the back, showing a vast under-dress hanging in folds of heavy satin.

And then I saw it! At the far side of the group was a slim, elegant figure dressed exactly like Kathleen. I hurried round to read the card. "Hobble Skirt, 1909-1913" was all it said.

"Well it might have told me something I don't already know," I said in disgust, still greatly fascinated by that particular style.

A moment later John came to look for me.

"You must be starving. Come and have some tea," he said.

And it was not until I was sitting at the table that I realised how hungry I was. As I ate, I made up my mind to see Miss Ormond as soon as possible—after tea if I could—and ask her to tell me more about the costume that Kathleen had been wearing.

Chapter 12

MISS ORMOND'S STORY

After tea I did slip up to Miss Ormond's room.

"I hear the fête's been a great success," she said, "and I'm so glad there's to be another dress and antique display. Fancy the contents of an old loft arousing such interest!"

"I'll tell you what interests me most, and that's Kathleen's costume," I said. "I wish I could wear it at the mannequin parade."

Miss Ormond's expression told me she did not approve of fashion parades.

"The shop will probably subscribe to the Rebuilding Fund," I added quickly.

"That's nice, but we're still nowhere near accepting Mr. Randall's offer," Miss Ormond replied. "It's very tantalising, but you see our plans for Oaklands have always looked a long way ahead. When I sold *Ormond Grange*, for instance, no one dreamed of the committee buying the site. Demolition costs alone would have ruled out that possibility."

"I do envy Kathleen displaying that hobble skirt," I said, changing the subject somewhat abruptly. "Can you tell me what they were for, Miss Ormond?"

"Hobble skirts? They weren't 'for' anything, my dear. It was no more than a fashion. Mind you, it was considered very smart to walk with tiny, lady-like steps, and those skirts allowed nothing else."

"Did you dress like that? I would have loved it!" I said.

"You can't put the clock back so don't think about it," Miss Ormond said. "And in any case I'm sure you wouldn't really have been happy in a hobble skirt. As the fashion caught on they became tighter and tighter. It was all right for rich ladies who had maids to wait on them and footmen to help them into their carriages, but ordinary people copied the fashion. Girls got into all sorts of difficulties and sometimes split their skirt seams."

"Did anything like that ever happen to you?" I asked.

"No, I took good care it didn't. I bought myself a costume that was to be the smartest ever, but I had the seams and hem specially strengthened to avoid splitting. It all came back to me when I saw Kathleen wearing it."

"You mean that two-piece was actually yours and you wore it all those years ago?" I said, my voice shrill with excitement.

"It was mine all right, but I didn't wear it much," Miss Ormond said. "Instead of being the smartest ever, it seemed the tightest ever. I called it my horrible hobble. When the fashion changed, my mother must have put it in the loft. She never threw anything away that wasn't worn out."

"I wouldn't have called it a horrible hobble. It looks so elegant, even today, that I wish it were mine," I persisted.

"You can't wear those clothes nowadays, you silly girl, but it would serve you right if you did have to dress like that," Miss Ormond said in a slightly scolding voice.

And then her manner changed and she began to talk very softly.

"Hugh didn't like that costume. At first he teased when I tried to keep up with him. He wasn't usually impatient but I seemed to make him so when I wore my hobble skirt. Perhaps he was embarrassed at having to almost lift me up steps and into buses. Poor, dear Hugh!"

I was bursting to ask who Hugh was, but I did not dare to interrupt.

"Yes, he was going to be ordained and then we planned to marry," Miss Ormond whispered, then suddenly she roused herself. "Dear me, what was I saying?" she asked.

"You were telling me about Hugh. Please go on."

"There's not much to tell, because our plans never came to anything. You see, Hugh was killed in France in the first World War. I thought I'd never bear the emptiness that came into my heart and life.... But why should I tell you this? It was all so long ago."

"I'm glad you have told me. I ... I know you'll understand how I feel about my mother."

And I blurted out all the things that were bottled up inside me—how much I loved Mummy, how I missed her and what a shock it was when she died. I also told Miss Ormond, somewhat fiercely, how wrong it was that Mummy should have died when she did.

"I remember John telling me of your mother's death, and I was grieved for you," Miss Ormond said. "And yet, you know, we must try not to question God's ways. It's so much easier if we believe that He makes no mistakes and that these sad things are allowed for a purpose."

"What sort of purpose is there in someone good getting ill and dying?" I asked, near to tears.

"I once felt just as you do," Miss Ormond replied gently, "but eventually I came to accept that Hugh's death was like a dark thread in the pattern of my life. I couldn't appreciate it, but God gave me the faith to believe that such darkness had been allowed only to show up a particularly beautiful part of His design."

"It would take faith to believe that all right!" I exclaimed. "I can't see that losing people you love does anyone any good."

"Well, maybe ... I don't know, but I sometimes think that the grief I suffered helped me to understand other people's troubles better," Miss Ormond said. "Certainly I could never share in the sorrows of others until I knew what sorrow was. But there, I'm trying to explain part of God's pattern, when one day the whole design will be plain to see."

John found me a silent companion on the way home that day because I was still thinking about what Miss Ormond had said. She, like John, talked about God as if He was someone she knew personally. Mummy used to talk about Him like that, too. When I was small she taught me to pray and told me that God would always hear and never be too busy to listen. I believed her in a childish sort of way, but after Mummy died I lost the vague faith I had in God. Now that I was older it was disturbing to find both John and Miss Ormond talking so naturally about Him. 'God makes no mistakes', Miss Ormond had said, as if nothing could shake her trust in Him.

The more I pondered over what Miss Ormond believed, the more I realised how different our ideas were. It was not only because she was elderly, either. Even when she was young she had overcome sorrow and bitterness and had devoted her life to helping others, especially the lonely, old ladies at Oaklands Home, and it had made her very sweet and contented.

"It's as if she's found some secret source of happiness that I know nothing of," I thought, "but perhaps that's because our ideas are so different."

But I did not face up completely to what the difference was. Had I done so, I would have realised that, whereas

Miss Ormond had devoted her life to helping others, my outlook was very selfish and self-centred. All I cared about was becoming a top model and making a name for myself. Whether I succeeded or not would depend upon me. Faith in God did not come into it.

Chapter 13

TWO KINDS OF TREASURE

The next day was Sunday and John asked me to go to church with him. I told him I would rather not. I always said that whenever he asked me.

"I was hoping you would come today because Pip's singing a solo," John said. "He's got a very nice voice, clear as a bell, with every note pure and true. You can hear the words plainly, too, even if you're sitting at the back of the church."

I would have liked to hear Pip sing, but I still made the excuse that I wanted to write a long letter to Daddy, telling him about the exhibition and how I wished he could have seen the things that were found in the loft.

After John had gone to church I almost wished I had agreed to go with him.

"Perhaps it's partly my fault we still aren't as close as we used to be," I thought. "But somehow we can't seem to help going off to follow our own interests. Maybe it's just that we're older and no longer want to play about all day the way we used to do."

Then, too, I reflected, it was surprising how much of the summer holiday had been swallowed up by the events at *Ormond Grange* and preparing for the fête and exhibition at Oaklands Old People's Home. All unnoticed, the days had gone slipping by. Soon the holiday would be over and I would say good-bye to John once again.

"I'll miss him, and yet he'd be a lot nicer if only he

didn't take religion so seriously," I thought, and then I got down to writing that letter to Daddy.

My pen was still skimming over the writing pad when John and his parents returned. They were amused when they saw what a wad I had written.

"Hey, you said a letter, not a book," John said, his eyes twinkling with amusement.

"I always write reams to Daddy," I replied. "How did the church service go?"

"Very well, and Pip sang better than ever," John told me. "There was a good sermon as well. The text was, 'Lay not up for yourselves treasures upon earth, where moth and rust doth corrupt ... but lay up for yourselves treasures in heaven, where neither moth nor rust doth corrupt ... for where your treasure is, there will your heart be also'."

"Oh yes," I said, rummaging about for an envelope.

"It reminded me of some of the things in those old trunks," John continued. "You know, the clothes that fell to bits when they were touched."

"But you'd hardly call them treasure," I objected, "—not a cloak and a soldier's uniform."

"No, but I meant as an example of what happens to all earthly things," John said. "The preacher told us that earthly treasure didn't necessarily mean riches. It could be fame, or anything that you set your heart on here. That's one reason why the Lord Jesus told His hearers not to set their hearts on earthly treasure. It doesn't last."

It was like being stabbed by a dart when John quoted *fame*. Why did he have to pick on that, of all things?—the one thing that my heart was set on!

"I can't see any point in being born if we can't enjoy ourselves and make the most of our lives," I retorted. "And what's treasure in heaven, anyway? How can you set your heart on something you can't be sure is really there?"

"Heavenly treasure is what Jesus will one day give to everyone who truly loves and serves Him," John explained. "The preacher said that no service, however small, will go unrewarded by treasure that will never perish. Even a cup of cold water given in Christ's name will have its reward."

I tried to shut my ears and my heart to what John had told me. Since I had been staying with him it had seemed more than once as if an invisible magnet was trying to draw me away from my own ideas and from what I intended to do with my life, and to make me think and live differently.

"It's all rubbish!" I said. "We're born to live in this world, not to be stuffing ourselves with thoughts of heaven. This is where my heart is, right here inside me," I added, thumping myself on the chest.

And how true that was, in more ways than one!

"If only you could see!" John replied.

I told him I had no intention of trying, and there the conversation lapsed.

I stuffed all the pages I had written to Daddy into a large envelope, sealed it with several loud thumps from my fist and stalked out of the room.

Chapter 14

A MYSTERIOUS TELEPHONE CALL

The telephone rang on Monday morning and I was surprised when Aunt Nancy said the call was for me. Surely it wasn't a long distance call from Daddy.

But when I picked up the phone it was Kathleen's voice I heard. She asked me to go to Oaklands that evening, but she would not say why. It all sounded very strange.

I was still puzzled when I walked up the Oaklands' driveway. Kathleen beckoned to me from a side door and led the way upstairs. She stopped on the landing and peeped into one of the rooms.

"There's a surprise for you to try on. Be careful; it's only tacked," she said, pushing me into the room.

Lying on a bed I saw a long, black velvet skirt.

"It's lovely," I exclaimed, "but why should anyone make it for me?"

Kathleen had slipped away so my question remained unanswered. I put the skirt on carefully, finding it rather strange to step into a full length skirt for the first time. It fitted very closely and when I looked into the wardrobe mirror it seemed to have made me inches taller.

Kathleen tapped on the door and came in with one of the Oaklands' residents.

"Doesn't she look a smasher, Mrs. Gordon?" Kathleen said, as she and the old lady smiled at one another, obviously enjoying my bewilderment.

Mrs. Gordon explained that Kathleen had told her how much I admired her two-piece and she, having been a dressmaker in her time, had the idea of making me a skirt like the one Kathleen had modelled.

"It's a sort of thank-you present," she went on. "You've worked hard for Oaklands and we didn't want you to feel left out of everything. You like it, don't you?"

"It's beautiful," I assured her, "but I don't know when I'll wear it."

"You're in Kennedy's fashion parade on Wednesday, love," Kathleen said. "It's all fixed. The compère says she can easily fit one more in."

I gaped at her, too thrilled and astonished to speak. Then I turned back to the mirror and tried to walk towards my own reflection.

"Isn't it tight! Supposing I split it?" I asked.

"Don't worry, dear," Mrs. Gordon said, smiling. "I've got this binding to go inside the hem."

She held up a circular band of strong linen tape and I was horrified to see how small it looked.

"Surely you must have got the measurement wrong!" I exclaimed.

Mrs. Gordon explained that Kathleen's skirt was almost a yard round the hem but mine was narrower because of the smaller size.

"It will be ready for you tomorrow evening," she added.

I was thrilled to bits about that skirt as I left Oaklands, and yet I was glad that Miss Ormond knew nothing about it. After what she had told me about her hobble skirt she would probably have thought I was crazy to want to appear in a fashion parade in one.

The next evening Kathleen handed me a neat parcel, saying how hard Mrs. Gordon had worked to get the skirt finished in time for the show. I asked Kathleen to thank her for me and hurried back to Uncle Jack's house, trembling with excitement. Tomorrow I would be a mannequin!

Before going to bed I tried the skirt on again. It fitted even more tightly now that the seams were finished and the zip fastener was in place. The hem was terribly narrow, but Kathleen had found a way to walk in hers so I would manage, too.

The next day Anna and I went to Kennedy's together. She had nothing to carry as Mr. Tomkinson was taking her dress in his van with the other costumes. I flatly refused to tell her what was in my parcel, remembering how she had teased Kathleen.

The van drew up just as we arrived and we watched Mr. Tomkinson and John carry a trunk and two cases into the store. Anna and I followed and found Susan and Kathleen already waiting. To my surprise, John stayed on after Mr. Tomkinson left. It was not like John to be interested enough to stay.

As we were last-minute additions to the show, we had only makeshift changing cubicles with nowhere to hang our own clothes. I wondered why we had been asked to come at ten when the parade did not start for another hour but Kathleen, who was sharing a cubicle with me, explained that the photographers were taking some pictures first. I thought they did that during the parade but Kathleen said it required a lot of time and patience to get a pose right, so the studio was the best place for it. She also told me that, as my skirt was not a genuine model, I would not be photographed. That was a big disappointment.

Before long, a superior-looking woman with a haughty expression looked into our cubicle.

"Your dresser will be along shortly," she said, and she promptly disappeared.

I waited impatiently, hardly believing that I really was going to take part in a fashion parade. I wondered, a little nervously, how I would manage since there had been so little opportunity to practise walking in the tight skirt.

Chapter 15

THE FASHION PARADE

"I'm blowed if I'm looking forward to this cat-walk business, but at least John will be a help," Kathleen said.

"John? How can he help?" I asked.

Kathleen surprised me further by saying that John had tried to borrow a young man's suit for the same period as her 'get-up' but Mr. Tomkinson could only let him have a footman's costume. He was wearing it specially to help Kathleen along the cat-walk.

"Real thoughtful, John is," she went on. "He knew I was only doing this for Oaklands and didn't want me bothered over it."

So that was why John was there. Fancy his being willing to appear in a fashion parade when he was not in the least interested in that sort of thing! Surprised as I was, I began to wish that he was helping me, too.

At last our dresser came.

"Sorry to keep you waiting," she said cheerily. "Had quite a job with your friend. Took two of us to get her laced up right."

As Kathleen was helped into her hobble skirt I noticed that the lace-fronted blouse she was wearing was a new one. It was brand-new yet it went perfectly with a suit over fifty years old! The dresser smoothed the skirt over Kathleen's hips and it was then that I saw it was too big at the waist, where the fastening overlapped badly.

"We'll have to do something about that," the dresser said, opening up a little hold-all, or 'first-aid kit' as she called it, and taking out a needle and thread.

"Don't sew me into this thing. That would be about the end!" Kathleen protested. "Can't you pin it?"

But the dresser was insistent, saying that she would get into trouble if she let a model appear with pins in her skirt.

"Supposing you had to open your jacket for the compère?" she asked.

"I don't want to get you into a row but it seems unusual . . ." Kathleen began.

"Unusual? It's not unusual at all," the dresser interrupted impatiently, already sewing up the overlap with neat, quick stitches.

"This is nothing to some of the things I have to do when a big display's on," she added. "We get broken zips, hooks missing, even split seams at times. My first-aid kit is invaluable!"

"But don't the models mind being sewn up?" Kathleen asked.

"Mind? They don't have to, but I guess they're too bored, anyway," the dresser replied, "particularly if they've done much photography work."

"Why should that make them bored?" I asked.

"Modelling's not much of a life and photographers don't always treat the models well," the dresser said. "Imagine posing for ages halfway down a flight of steps while somebody keeps fiddling with your clothes. It's no joke."

"And *you* want to be a model!" Kathleen said.

At that moment we heard Anna giggling outside, and then Susan appeared asking for Kathleen to go with them to the studio. We discovered that the dresser was called Kathleen, too, and she chuckled as she helped our Kathleen into her close-fitting jacket and set her wide-brimmed hat at exactly the right angle.

"I'm glad I'm not the Kathleen that's got to walk to the studio in that skirt," she said.

She then asked me where the other dresses came from. As she helped me into my long, black skirt I told her that they were genuine period costumes discovered at *Ormond Grange*. I was relieved that my skirt fastened properly but the dresser disappointed me by saying that the zip showed badly and spoilt the line. Remembering how she had spoken to Kathleen I did not dare to protest as she sewed me up, too. When she had finished, the material lay as flat as a properly finished seam.

"When I leave school I want to model for a Paris designer so I suppose I'll have to get used to this sort of thing," I told her.

"You want to be a model? Well, I hope you won't be as disillusioned as a friend of mine who modelled for a Paris fashion house. She found the competition frightful and it was terribly hard work."

"I wouldn't mind those things; I'd be too thrilled," I declared.

"Get away with you. Models have to stand for hours on end while the couturier works on the shaping of one dress after another, and there's endless try-ons and alterations. By the time the collection is ready for showing, the models are practically dead on their feet. Then there's the private shows, photographers, fashion artists, buyers ... it's a non-stop slog."

"But just think of wearing such exclusive dresses and having your picture on the covers of glossy magazines!"

"You're obviously incurable," the dresser said, as she left.

I noticed that our Kathleen had put her ordinary clothes in her case so I folded up my own skirt and put it with them. Next I tried to sit down, only to find I could hardly bend. Sitting down proved both difficult and uncomfortable. Miss Ormond had not mentioned that problem!

It was all quiet outside so I practised walking along the corridor instead. I did not get on very well so I lifted the skirt to stop the hem pulling on my ankles, but that did not help because then my knees knocked together and I could not walk at all. I was still trying to get the hang of it when I heard the other three returning from the studio.

Susan was complaining of hardly being able to breathe and she was still upset about the way the dressers had tugged and pulled at her corset lacing.

"I think they're cruel; they seemed to enjoy it," she said.

"Perhaps they're jealous. They must wish they could be models," I replied.

"I'd much rather be myself and be able to breathe and walk without difficulty," Kathleen said, giving me a black look.

Susan slipped quietly back to her cubicle with Anna, leaving Kathleen and me in an awkward silence that seemed to last for ages. I didn't even dare to ask why they had been so long at the photographers. Eventually Susan and Anna re-appeared, dressed in their own clothes.

"What's happened? Is the show over?" Kathleen asked impatiently.

"Of course not. We were on early; it's your turn soon," Susan replied.

Then the haughty woman in charge of the gown department told us to hurry to the stage. John was already there, wearing a white wig, green velvet coat and breeches, white stockings and black, buckled shoes. Kathleen held on to his arm gratefully and they looked terrific as they stepped onto the stage together. John bowed deeply, took Kathleen's outstretched hand and led her to the cat-walk out of my sight. I heard loud applause and cries of 'Bravo' as they returned gratefully to the stage; then it was my turn.

I walked slowly forward, carefully edging one foot in front of the other, and tried to curtsy to the compère.

"I was wondering how today's teenagers would get on in skirts that length," the compère said, as Kathleen and John stepped back in mock surprise. "Now, my dear, let's see what you can do."

With a sweep of his arm, John waved me towards the cat-walk. Evidently there was no help for me, so I started off alone. Taking only small steps, I found that I could not move my arms in rhythm with my pace. Instead, I put one hand on my hip and tried to assume the aloof air of a professional model. At last I reached the end of the cat-walk and turned delicately. As I started back, two ladies in the front row giggled and I panicked. I tried to hurry past them but the narrow hem jerked round my ankles and brought me to a halt. I began again, more steadily, and it was with relief that I walked off the stage, glad that I had not fallen down but disappointed with my first show.

Kathleen was very pleased it was all over, even smiling a little as we waited to be cut free so that we could change into our own clothes. Unfortunately, we could not find our dresser anywhere and Susan was still looking for her when a secretary appeared and told us that the store manager wanted to see the Oaklands' girls in his office.

Neither Kathleen nor I wanted to walk another step dressed like that but, as the minutes ticked by and we still could not change, the manager's secretary became very worried and practically insisted that we should come as we were.

Susan thought it would be bad for Oaklands if we kept the manager waiting after the way he had publicised our exhibition in his store. She made up our minds for us by taking Kathleen firmly by the arm and leading her off; the secretary took my arm, too, and I found it was a choice between following or falling over, so I followed.

When we reached the manager's office we found he was a charming man. He thanked us for taking part in the parade, and he produced some large photographs.

"What do you think of yourselves?" he asked, passing the pictures to Kathleen and Susan, who were surprised to be shown proofs of the photographs taken before the show.

I saw that the first one was of Anna. She looked sweet in the white party dress, not at all like the tomboy she really was. Suddenly I felt uneasy. Anna should have been with us in the manager's office but she was nowhere about when we came and I wondered where she was now.

The next picture was of Susan in her ball gown, and it showed up beautifully. There were several photos of Kathleen. One shot showed clearly how the hobble skirt narrowed to her knees and ended in a straight tube to her ankles.

"No wonder it doesn't lift, shaped like that," I thought, feeling quite cross with the designer, whoever he might have been. "If I'd been his model I'd have refused to wear it."

Then I remembered something the dresser had told me.

"Competition's so keen that no model dare so much as criticise her designer's creations, otherwise she is 'out' and someone else takes her place," she had said.

I made up my mind there and then that that wouldn't happen to me, no matter what I had to put up with. In spite of my disappointment I felt that I had learned a lot that morning.

Suddenly I came back to earth. The manager was bidding us good-bye, and a moment later Kathleen and I were hobbling back to our changing room and our own clothes at last—or so we thought.

Chapter 16

A WRITTEN NAME

When Kathleen and I got back to our cubicle we were horrified to find our case had vanished. Before we had recovered from the shock the haughty-looking woman appeared with a message for us.

"Your friends have gone off with the cases in the van," she said. "They couldn't wait for you because of the fifteen minute parking limit."

"But our clothes! What on earth shall we do?" Kathleen said.

"Now what's the matter?" the woman asked crossly, turning to Susan.

"All my friends want is their own clothes," Susan replied, doing her best to sound polite.

"Well, there's nothing I can do about that," said the woman, looking us up and down with an amused smirk. "They'll have to go home as they are."

And away she stalked, leaving us to sort things out for ourselves.

"So much for the way models get treated," Kathleen said in disgust. "As far as she's concerned, we might as well be a couple of coathangers!"

"Come on, hurry up," Susan said. "We're supposed to be helping with the mid-day meal."

Kathleen was furious and refused to leave until somebody released her. It was obvious that no one in the store would help and she finally agreed, very reluctantly, to try and get back to Oaklands in the hobble skirt.

It was terribly difficult, picking our way along the busy streets, taking tiny, little steps, and Kathleen grumbled all the way to the bus stop. She was blaming John but it was not fair as he had really tried to be helpful. When the bus came we could not even get up the step and Susan had to lift us.

We could not sit properly, either, and we were glad to get off that bus. It was still a long walk to Oaklands, quite the worst part of our trip, and Susan left us to it. I tried to tell Kathleen how elegant she looked in her suit and the wide-brimmed hat, hoping to cheer her up, but just then an errand boy whistled at us as we hobbled past. That upset Kathleen once more. The farther we went the more irritable she became, and I knew only too well the reason why. Wearing a long, slim skirt in the store was bad enough, but having to walk the best part of a mile home was ten times worse.

"I suppose you're happy now, aren't you? This is what you wanted, isn't it?" Kathleen snapped.

I tried to tell her that of course it wasn't, but it was no use. She wanted to blame John or Anna or me, and I was nearest.

"People who followed fashions like this must have been mad," she went on. "What was the point of it all?"

I was lost for an answer and remained silent, but Kathleen kept on grumbling. If there had been any way of splitting the hem of her skirt, I knew she would have done it, but the binding was too strong.

"Miss Ormond wore that suit when she was young and considered it very smart," I said.

"Smart! Smart! That's all your head's full of," Kathleen exploded. "If you still want to press on with your modelling after this morning's 'do', you're welcome."

I did not admit it to Kathleen, but in my own heart I knew I wanted to be a famous model more than anything else in the world. It would be harder work than I had imagined, but I was determined, whatever the cost, that I would climb to the top of fashion's ladder to fame.

We struggled on in silence until at last we reached Oaklands.

"Here's our case, so that's something to be thankful for," Kathleen said, as we hobbled into the hall.

I took my clothes and went slowly up the staircase, just managing one step at a time. On the landing I met Miss Ormond on her way down to lunch. She looked at me in astonishment as I did my best to hurry past. To be seen by her in such a predicament was the last thing I wanted.

I changed quickly, snipping recklessly at the stitches that had imprisoned me in the hobble skirt. It was a relief to wear my own clothes once more and to be able to run downstairs to help Susan and Kathleen catch up with their work.

After lunch I was busy clearing the plates away when Miss Ormond touched me lightly on the arm.

"I know you're busy now, my dear," she said, "but I would like to see you when you have more time."

Miss Ormond's invitation was very welcome. I was so bewildered when I looked back on the morning's events and my peep behind the fashion world scenes, that I wanted to talk to someone about it all. I slipped away as soon as I could and Miss Ormond pulled up a chair by the window for me.

"Helen, dear, I heard about the skirt that Mrs. Gordon made for you," Miss Ormond began. "I hoped you wouldn't wear it at the fashion parade, but I never thought you would go as far as walking home in it. Forgive me if I'm interfering, but I feel that at least Kathleen should have known better. Couldn't you see that you were only making an exhibition of yourselves?"

"Oh, but you don't understand. It was all a terrible mix-up," I explained.

And I went on to tell her what had happened. I also told her that, in spite of everything I had seen and heard at the fashion parade, I still intended to become a model.

"I know it will be hard work, but I don't mind as long as I succeed and become really famous in the end," I said.

Miss Ormond looked at me sadly, but there was nothing condemning about her attitude so I tried to explain more clearly how I felt.

"You see, ever since Mummy died I've been terribly uncertain about life," I said. "So many things could happen. I could be run over or there could be a dreadful atomic war. As soon as I get the chance I want to make a name for myself."

"But, my dear girl, you could find it so disappointing," Miss Ormond said gently. "If I may, I'd like to tell you about something that happened to me a long time ago, when I was younger than you are now. My parents took me on my first visit to the seaside and I was charmed by the beautiful shells on the shore. One day I collected a lot and spelt out my name in the sand with them. When I had finished I was pleased that the folk on the promenade could read my name as they passed. It made me feel proud and important. The next day I ran down to the shore specially to look at my name, only to find that the tide had washed it away."

"What a sad, little story," I said.

"Yes, in a way, and yet it afterwards taught me something I've never forgotten," Miss Ormond went on. "You see, if our aim in life is to make a name for ourselves here, we're going to be sadly disappointed because the names of today are forgotten by tomorrow. But if we have our names written in heaven, that's a very different thing. God never forgets us and when we die He welcomes us to live with Him for ever."

I was surprised by what Miss Ormond told me.

"But how can you get your name written in heaven?" I asked.

"There's a special book called the Lamb's book of life," she said. "It belongs to the Lord Jesus, God's spotless Lamb Who offered Himself as a sacrifice for our sins. If we come to Him and accept the salvation He offers, then He writes our name in His book, and there it stays until we join Him in heaven."

I was disturbed as well as surprised by what Miss Ormond said. It reminded me of what John had once told me about the special mansions that Jesus was preparing for those who love Him. But what about me? I knew there could not be a room in one of those mansions for me. And what about the names written in heaven? I knew mine was not among them.

Miss Ormond sat quietly with her eyes half closed and her delicate hands resting on her lap. She looked as if she had forgotten I was there and was having a lovely daydream about heaven.

"But surely there's nothing wrong with being a model?" I said. "It isn't a sin to love nice clothes, is it?"

"I didn't say it was," Miss Ormond replied, her blue eyes fully opened once more. "It's more a matter of what we put first in our lives, and the world of fashion is so fleeting. That doesn't mean there's anything wrong with being neatly or even smartly dressed or in being interested in design and so on. But to centre your life on modelling, in the hope of making a name for yourself, that could bring bitter disillusionment. Think about what I've said, my dear. Only you can decide whether you would prefer your name to be written in heaven or on earth."

All at once it was as if *my* eyes had been half closed, but now I could see clearly. I realised that ever since my mother died I had shut God completely out of my life—indeed He had never had much of a place before that. I saw my sinfulness and self-will. As for what the Lord Jesus had suffered that I might be forgiven and have eternal life, I had never given it a thought.

But now I sat perfectly still and thought a lot about it. In the end I made a terribly important decision. I decided that my name should be written in heaven and not on earth. There, in Miss Ormond's little room, I covered my face with my hands and offered myself to the Lord Jesus, asking Him to forgive me for all the wrong, selfish things I had thought and done.

Miss Ormond understood exactly what had happened and held out her arms to me. In a second I was kneeling at her feet, crying for joy. It was a great relief to cry like that. Those tears washed away a whole load of bitterness and resentment from my heart.

When I left Oaklands I was filled with a peace and happiness that I could never express in words. Life had taken on a new meaning. It had a worthwhile purpose and an end that would never end, as you might say. From now on I would try to live in the way that my Saviour wanted me to, leaving the actual pattern of my life for Him to reveal. Then, one day, I would go home to be with Him for ever. It was hard to take in the wonder of it all.

That night I lay in bed and tried to imagine what it would be like—heaven in the presence of the Lamb of God who had died for me, and where Miss Ormond would be re-united with Hugh and I would see Mummy again. There would be no more parting for any of us and no more pain or sickness. Instead, we would be completely happy in the mansions that the Lord Jesus had prepared for us, for John and his parents and for everyone else who truly loves Him. Yes, it was hard to take in the wonder and joy of it all!

Chapter 17

A DAY OF GOOD NEWS

The next morning I woke up with a feeling of deep, inner happiness that I knew I could share with John. When I told him that I had given my heart and life to the Lord Jesus, his face lit up with joy—even though he did chide me a little for not telling him the day before.

"So there will be room in a heavenly mansion for both of us after all," I said. "I wish I knew more about those mansions. Suddenly they seem so real and wonderful."

John smiled and said that the Bible tells us so many of God's secrets and plans that we mustn't grumble if He's kept a few back as an extra special surprise.

After breakfast we went to *Ormond Grange* together, or rather to the site where the Grange used to be, and found that Pip and Anna also had some good news to share with us. Pip said that the Taylors would not be moving to Barfold after all. He looked quite his old self as he told us about it. His Dad, he said, had not been offered that job but he had found himself a part-time one nearer home. It was only a temporary answer to their problem, but at least they would be staying where they were a little longer.

"And Mokey will be staying, too," Anna added.

Looking back, it seems there was no end to the good news that day and I must try to keep everything in the right order. The next thing that happened after we had heard Pip's news was that my father came to the Grange looking for me.

"Daddy!" I cried. "I thought you were still in Florence."

"I flew back yesterday," he said.

"And was it a successful trip?" John asked.

"Not as successful as some, but we mustn't grumble," Daddy told him.

"But what about my letter?" I asked. "I wrote you simply reams on Sunday."

"Sorry, darling, but my post hasn't caught up with me yet so you'll have to tell me all the news," Daddy said. "I specially want to know what's happened to the treasure trove you told me about in your previous letter."

Telling was not enough, so that afternoon I took Daddy to Oaklands to see the exhibition. To my disappointment, Mr. Tomkinson had taken most of the things away, but there were still some paintings left. Daddy looked at them closely and asked me if there were any more. When I told him that the curator had kept several at the museum, he was so keen to see them that he hired a taxi and went off at once. And that was the start of something almost too good to be true.

While Daddy was at the museum I went to see Miss Ormond and we talked together until he came back. As soon as he returned he told her that several of her long-forgotten pictures were nineteenth century originals, some of them belonging to the early French Impressionist period and worth a great deal of money. He was sure one painting alone would sell for fifteen thousand pounds!

Miss Ormond took this news surprisingly calmly, asking Daddy to take complete charge of the pictures and to sell them as soon as possible.

"I need the money for something special," she explained.

"Miss Ormond, you will be positively rich!" I said, unable to keep a shrill note of excitement from my voice.

"My dear, this is such a wonderful answer to prayer," she replied. "The money will pay for the building of a beautiful new home. I shall tell Oaklands Committee to accept Mr. Randall's offer at once."

"You ... you mean you're going to give it all away?" I stammered.

"Why, Helen, you already know where my heart and true treasure lie, don't you? I couldn't do anything better with the money than give it away."

Miss Ormond's words sobered me strangely. I realised how absolutely sincere she was. She had already told me that her treasure was in heaven and now, had I needed proof, I could actually see it was true. She had no heart for earthly wealth, except to do good with it.

As the full importance of her decision dawned on me I prayed a quick prayer that when my new-found faith was put to the test, in whatever form that test should take, I would be as unwavering as Miss Ormond.

Events moved swiftly and not many days passed before Mr. Taylor had agreed to stay on at Ormond Lodge while the new Old People's Home was being built, possibly helping the site foreman and generally keeping the grounds as tidy as he could.

"Daddy says there'll be enough money to build a few little bungalows for old ladies who can look after themselves, so this estate will probably be re-named Ormond Old People's Village," I told Pip and Anna. "There'll be a big house for those who need caring for and the bungalows will be behind it, maybe built in fours among the apple trees."

"And I know something you don't," Pip added. "We're having a special bungalow built for us down by the paddock and Daddy's staying here as groundsman and general handyman, just like he used to be."

It was marvellous the way everything was working out

and so much to grasp all at once, that the four of us lay quietly in the orchard, trying to take in all that had happened during that eventful summer holiday. Even Anna was silent, though not for long. She called us over to look at 'something queer' that was happening on a twig. We wriggled closer and watched a butterfly emerge from its chrysalis. It climbed slowly to a leafy sprig, where it hung upside down. Even as we watched, its wings seemed to grow. We were fascinated by the way they gradually spread and lost their creases. At last a fully developed tortoiseshell took flight and we watched it mount up above the apple trees and disappear into the blue.

'Oh! Wasn't that lovely?" Anna gasped.

"It's almost like a symbol," John said slowly. "Just think; that butterfly was once an ugly caterpillar, but it turned into a chrysalis, almost a dead thing, and today it emerged, becoming a lovely creature of the sun and air with a much better life than it had before."

"Why's it a symbol?" Anna asked, with a puzzled frown.

"I was going to say, in a way it's a symbol or picture of what's happened to *Ormond Grange*. It was an old house, shabby and worn out, and so it died. Yet, you see, like the caterpillar, it 'died' for a purpose. Its place will be taken by something far better—a beautiful, little village that will give happiness to many people."

Anna clapped her hands excitedly.

"So it didn't matter about the old house dying, after all, did it?" she said. "Helen looks all dreamy. I don't think she's listening."

"Oh yes, I am," I told her. "I was thinking of what John said about that butterfly. It reminds me of something even more wonderful than a house dying and living again. I'm thinking of what will happen to us when we go to heaven. Miss Ormond told me the Bible says that, if we believe on the Lord Jesus, one day we'll have new bodies. We can't imagine what they'll be like, but it will be more marvellous than a caterpillar changing into a butterfly."

"It's grand to know that you believe these things at last," John said, putting his hands on my shoulders and smiling down at me. "It's right what it says in the front of Miss Ormond's old Bible. Do you remember, Helen?"

"Unto God, Who is able to do exceeding abundantly above all that we ask or think," we said together.